COVENANT

for

Kids!

Written by: Lacie Wright

© 2008 by Lacie Wright. Revised 2011. All rights reserved.
Covenant for Kids! Student Workbook

Unless otherwise noted all Scripture quotations are from the New American Standard Bible, ©1960, 1962, 1963, 1968, 1971, 1972, 1973, 1975, 1977, by The Lockman Foundation. Used by permission.

Where noted Scripture taken from The Message, ©1993, 1994, 1995, 1996, 2000, 2001, 2002. Used by permission of NavPress Publishing Group.

ISBN: 978-0-6152-0658-5

TABLE OF CONTENTS

What is Covenant? 4

Friends Forever
     Jonathan 7
     David 11
     Jonathan & David's Covenant 15

God's Covenants
     Noah 22
     Abraham 25
     Jacob 27
     Children of Israel 31

Law: The Old Covenant 34

Grace: The New Covenant 41

Our Part in Covenant 50

Conclusion 52

~INTRODUCTION~

Have you ever written a note to your best friend? It was probably full of secrets that only the two of you knew. You may have included jokes or stories that only your friend would be able to share with you.

Similarly, the Bible is God's special letter to His friends—us! To write this letter to us, He used a special language called **Covenant**. By studying this language of covenant, we will be able to understand the meaning in God's letter to us!

~DEFINITION~

To begin with, we first have to find out **what exactly is covenant**?
In the Hebrew language, the word _berîyth_ is used. But what does that mean?
First, use your dictionary to look up the word _covenant_ and write what you discover below:

_____

_____

According to the Hebrew transliteration, "**covenant**" is a "treaty, an alliance of friendship, a pledge. . . contract which was accompanied by signs, sacrifices, and a solemn oath which sealed the relationship with promises of blessing for obedience and curses for disobedience."[1] This certainly sounds like an important word, doesn't it!?

---

1. Spiros Zodhiates, *Hebrew Greek Key Word Study Bible, New American Standard Version, Old Testament Lexical Aids*, (Chattanooga: TN: AMG Publishers, 1990), #1285.

Do you have any people in your life now with whom you have made a lifelong promise of friendship? _____
_____

Long ago, people would enter into these agreements or covenants by making a solemn vow or promise. This was not a promise that they took lightly. In fact to show their seriousness in making this promise, they would make some kind of a **sign** to symbolize the covenant. For example, the partners in covenant would cut their wrists and then grasp each other's arms so that their blood joined and they became blood brothers. Symbolically, they were becoming one person. This meant that they were now bound to one another. Because of this covenant, they could no longer be selfish or self-seeking. Each partner would act in a way that would benefit and protect the other.

Another characteristic of covenant is **sacrifice**. The partners making covenant would sacrifice, or kill, animals which was a way of saying to each other "if I break this vow, I deserve to die like these animals". Wow! Covenant really sounds like a serious thing!

- *Can you imagine being in an agreement like that?* _____

- *Do you think it would be easy to think of another person in every decision you make?*
_____

What is Covenant?

On this page, draw a picture of your best friend or friends. Make it colorful and make sure it really reflects their personality!

FRIENDS FOREVER: JONATHAN & DAVID

A perfect example of this kind of friendship can be found in the story of David and Jonathan.

JONATHAN

Let's start by getting some background on both of these young men.

1 Samuel 14:1 - Jonathan was the son of _____

And who was Saul?

1 Samuel 15:1—Saul is the _____ over _____

So this means that Jonathan is what? _____

Now, both father and son were warriors who often went into battle against the Lord's enemies. Let's compare and contrast these two men.

In **1 Samuel 14**, Jonathan goes to fight the Philistines with only 1 other person to help him. Look at what he says in verse 6:

"Come and let us _____ over to the garrison of these uncircumcised; perhaps the _____ will _____ for us, for the _____ is not _____ to save by many or by few."

So what does this tell you about Jonathan's character? _____
_____

Verse 45-   Who won the battle? _____

                Did God come through for Jonathan? _____

We see that Jonathan displayed courage and trust in God when he battled the Philistines. However, Israel had another enemy, the Amalekites.

> Read **1 Samuel 15** and mark the following key words: obey, reject

The Amalekites had been enemies of Israel for a while. In fact, go to **Deuteronomy 25:17-19** and read about these people.

- According to this passage, what kinds of things did the Amalekites do to the Israelites? _____
  _____

- What was Israel told to do to them? _____
  _____

Look at what you read in **1 Samuel 15**. God gave Saul very specific instructions about what to do to the Amalekites.

Verse 3- Saul is told to "go and _____ Amalek and utterly _____ all that he has and do not _____ him; but put to _____ both man and woman, child and infant, ox and sheep, camel and donkey."

Does Saul obey the Lord's instructions (verse 9)? _____

Verse 11- God says that He _____ making Saul king for "he has _____ back from _____ Me, and has _____ carried out My _____."

So Saul was given specific instructions to follow. Does he follow those instructions? _____ What is this called? _____

✤ What are the consequences for Saul's disobedience (verse 26)?

The Lord has _____ him from being king over Israel.

Can you imagine what it would feel like to know you've been rejected by God!?

_____

What does this show you about how God feels about obedience? Is it ok to only obey half of what you're told to do?

_____

_____

_____

Let's fill in what we've learned so far about this father and son. How are they similar? How are they different?

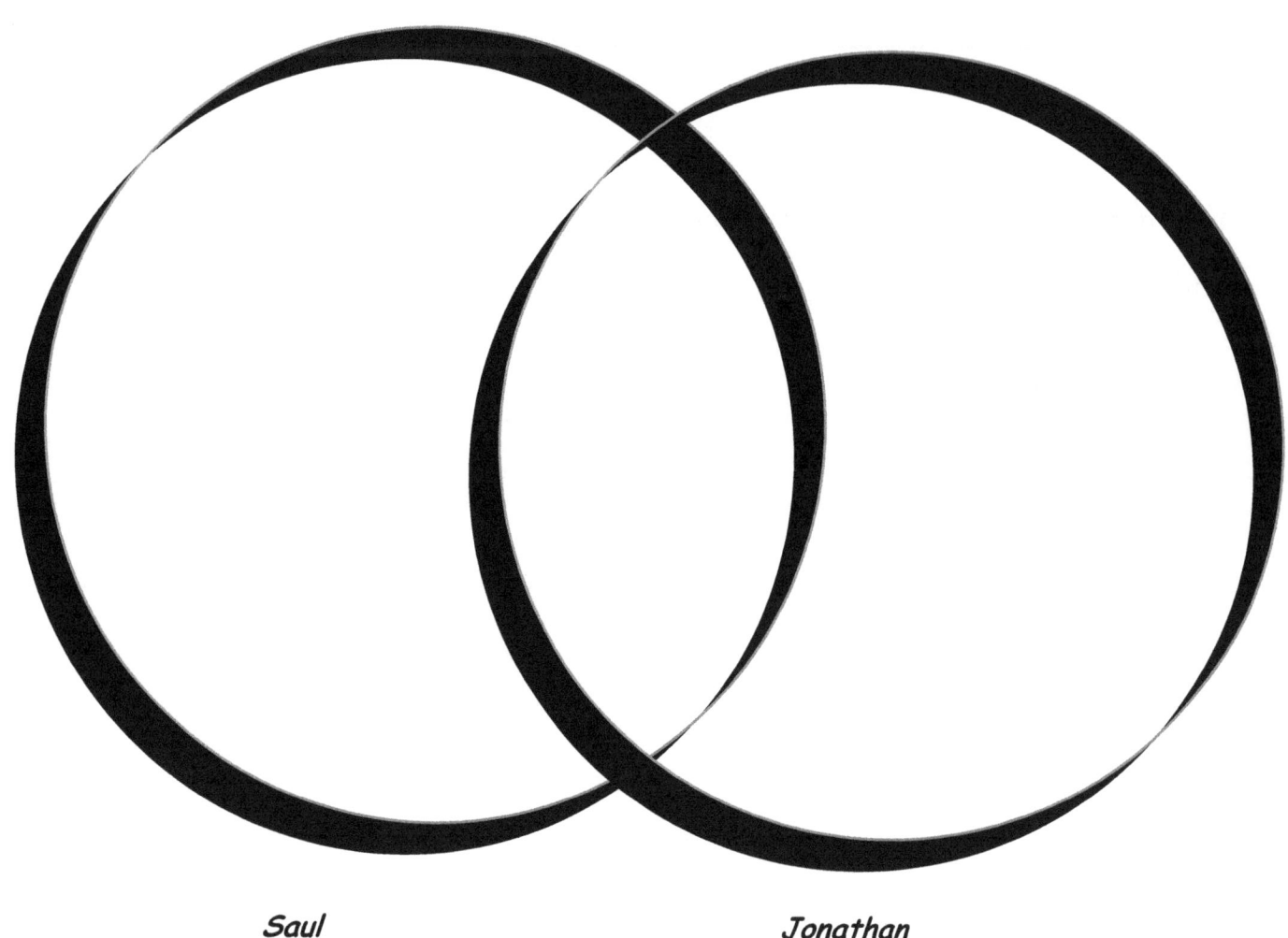

Saul   Jonathan

~DAVID~

Now, let's see what we can find out about David, the boy who would become the best friend of the Prince of Israel.

We learned already that God was no longer happy with Saul because of his disobedience. In fact, He was so displeased that He decided to find a new king for Israel. Go to **1 Samuel 16** to see what happens next!

1 Samuel 16:1 God tells Samuel to "_____ your horn with _____ and go; I will send you to _____ the Bethlehemite, for I have_____ a _____ for Myself among his _____."

Verse 11   What was David's job?   _____

Verses 12-13 Who is the son of Jesse that Samuel anoints as the next king of Israel?
_____

Let's try to get a little more detail about David. Look at **1 Samuel 16:12** for a description of his appearance.

David is described as: _____.

Verse 18 describes him as well: ". . . a _____ of Jesse the Bethlehemite who is a _____ _____, a _____ _____of _____, a _____, one_____in _____, and a _____ man; and the _____ is_____him.

What was it about David that caused God to select him as the next king? _____
_____

What does this tell you about God? What is important to Him? _____

_____

_____

Not long after David is anointed by Samuel, Israel is terrorized by the Philistines and their champion, Goliath. Go read **1 Samuel 17:31-37** to see how David handles himself in this battle.

Verse 32- David tells King Saul that he will _____ and _____ with this Philistine.

Verses 34-37—What two things did David kill while tending his father's sheep?

_____.

✤ So what kinds of character qualities do we see in David from these passages? ____

_____

Fill in the blanks from **verses 45-46** to see who David is trusting in for victory over Goliath.

Then David said to the Philistine, "You come to me with a _____, a _____, and a _____, but I come to you in the _____ of the _____ of hosts, the God of the _____ of _____, whom you have taunted. This day the _____ will deliver you up into my_____, and I will _____you down….that all the earth may know that there is a _____ in Israel…"

12

Friends Forever: David

Verse 47- "...for the battle is the _____ and He will _____ you into our _____."

✢ Does David's response remind you of anyone else we've learned about? _____
_____

Verse 50— Who wins the battle? _____

Let's compare and contrast David and Jonathan. What kinds of things have you learned that these 2 young men have in common? How are they different?

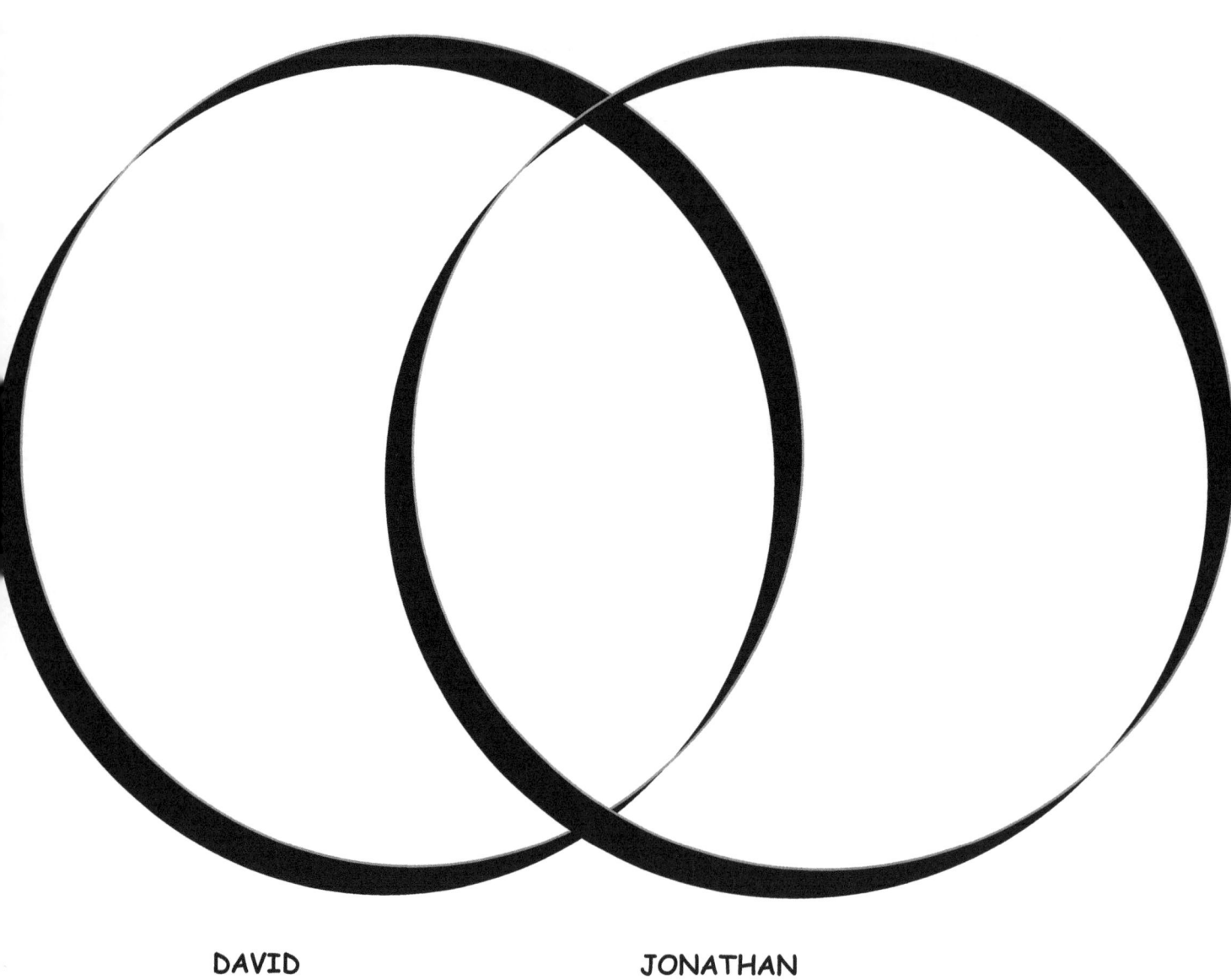

DAVID   JONATHAN

Jonathan & David's Covenant

COVENANT

So, now you've gotten a picture of what kind of men David and Jonathan are. Now let's look at their relationship.

> Read **I Samuel 18:1-9** and mark the following key words: **David, Jonathan, Saul, love, hate, covenant**

Verse 1- Jonathan's _____ was knit to the soul of _____ and Jonathan _____him as himself.

The Hebrew word for *knit* is **qashar**. This means "to bind up. . . conspire. . . join together, knit." [1]

This idea of being knit together and loving someone as yourself sounds like something you've learned already, doesn't it? What word have you learned that represents an unselfish friendship and promise? _____!

Verse 3- Jonathan made a _____ with David. Why does Jonathan make a covenant with David? _____.

Interesting! Did David do anything to earn Jonathan's love? Did he have to be the best at everything to make Jonathan love him? No! Jonathan chose to love David. And because he loved him, he chose to enter into a covenant with David!

Verse 4- To show his covenant with David, Jonathan gives David some things:

_____

---

1. Spiros Zodhiates, *Hebrew Greek Key Word Study Bible, New American Standard Version*, Hebrew Dictionary, (Chattanooga: TN: AMG Publishers, 1996) #7194

Jonathan & David's Covenant

Jonathan was the Prince of Israel! Draw a picture below of what you think his royal robe and armor would have looked like:

Robe	**Armor**

Do you realize that as Saul's son, Jonathan would likely have become king after his father? But remember, Saul's disobedience has cost him the throne and instead a shepherd boy has been anointed the future King of Israel.

Imagine that you are Jonathan and your throne and inheritance has been given to a shepherd boy who is not even related to you! How would you feel about David if you were in Jonathan's position? _____

_____

But **1 Samuel 18:1** told us that Jonathan loved David as himself! Jonathan, the Prince of Israel, gives up his royalty, his robe and armor to this boy who has been anointed the next King of Israel. This shows us an important character quality of Jonathan: **humility**.

What is **humility**? Use your dictionary to look up this word and write the definition here: _____

_____

We see that Jonathan is more concerned with obeying God than he is about preserving his own position as prince.

So Jonathan gave up his robe and his armor when he entered into covenant to David. Why do you think he did this? Go back and look again at the definition of covenant on page 4. We said that when you enter into covenant with someone, you become _____ with them. So when Jonathan gave David his robe he was symbolically taking off his identity as prince and giving it to David! We also learned that when you enter into covenant with someone, you are vowing to protect and defend them.

Fill in what you've learned:

Jonathan gives 2 things to David: **This represents:**

1. _____   _____

2. _____   _____

Now, let's get back to the story! Prince Jonathan has just made covenant with the shepherd boy who has been anointed the next King of Israel. But don't forget—Saul is still king. And he is *not* happy about David's anointing!

Jonathan & David's Covenant

In fact, Saul tries on several occasions to kill David.

> Read **1 Samuel 20** to hear what happens next. Be sure to mark key words: **Jonathan, David, Saul, God, swear, love, hate.**

Now let's answer a few questions about what you've read to see what happens between our two heroes, Jonathan and David.

Verses 1-3 What is David's mood like? _____

Verses 6-7 David asks Jonathan to test Saul to see if he does really intend to kill David. He tells Jonathan to say that he has gone to what city? _____. And if Saul is unhappy about David leaving, this will show Jonathan and David that Saul intends to do what? _____

Because Jonathan is Saul's son, David realizes that Jonathan could very well choose to side with his father. But in verse 8, David asks Jonathan to "deal _____ with thy servant for thou has brought thy servant into a _____ of _____ with thee..."

How does Jonathan answer? _____
_____

In **verse 13**, Jonathan makes another vow to David: "If it please my _____ to do you harm, may the _____ do so to _____ and more also, if I do not make it known to you and _____ you away that you may go in _____. And may the _____ be with _____ as He _____ been with my _____."

18

Jonathan & David's Covenant

✦ Based on this verse, whose side do you think Jonathan is on?

_____

Verses 14-15   "And if I am still _____ will you not show me the _____ of the Lord; that I may not die? And you shall not _____ off your _____ from my _____ forever, not even when the Lord cuts off every one of the _____ of David from the face of the earth."

✦ Who is talking here? _____

✦ Why do you think Jonathan says "if I am still alive"? _____

_____

Verse 17   "And _____ made _____ vow again because of his _____ for him, because he _____ him as he _____ his own _____."

So again Jonathan and David make a covenant and vow to protect and take care of one another. But notice that Jonathan asks David to show lovingkindness to his house as well. This is characteristic of covenants. When you enter into covenant with someone, you vow to treat their friends and family as well as you treat them. Jonathan understands this and wants to be sure that even though he will not become King, his family will be taken care of.

The two men come up with a way to get word to David if Saul reacts violently to the news that David has gone to Bethlehem. Look at verses 19-22 and write down what their plan is: _____

_____

_____

✦ Is Saul angry that David is gone? (verse 30) _____

✦ Who does Saul take his anger out on? (verse 33)_____

✦ How does Jonathan react to this news? (verse 34) _____
_____

✦ Does Jonathan keep his word to David and warn him about the danger? (verse 35)
_____

After Jonathan sends the armor bearer to get his arrows, he sends him away so that he can quietly say goodbye to his best friend. Have you ever had a best friend who moved away and you had to say goodbye to them? Do you remember how you felt? If you do, then you probably have a good idea of the way Jonathan and David were feeling.

Let's take a minute to look at their goodbye:

Verse 41 "When the lad had gone, _____ rose from the south side and fell on his to the ground, and _____ three times. And they kissed each other and_____ together, but _____ more."

Verse 42 And _____ said to _____, "Go in _____, inasmuch as we have _____to each other in the _____of the Lord, saying 'The _____will be _____me and you, and between my _____and your _____ forever'..."

✦ What are the 2 friends saying here? Put it in your words: _____
_____
_____
_____

Jonathan & David's Covenant

By looking at the story of Jonathan and David's friendship, we have learned what covenant is and what it is meant to do. Let's review the characteristics of covenant.

1. What is the definition of covenant? _____
_____
_____

2. Signs or symbols often accompanied covenant. What's an example of a sign of covenant?
_____
_____
_____

3. Sacrificing an animal when you enter covenant meant what? _____
_____
_____

4. Write out a prayer to God here to tell Him how you're feeling about what you've learned so far. Do you want to know more? Ask Him to show you all He has for you!

_____
_____
_____
_____
_____

GOD'S COVENANTS

~NOAH~

So now that you understand what a covenant is and what it meant, let's look at some of the covenants God made. That's right, the God of the universe actually entered into covenant with people He chose!

> The first covenant recorded in the Bible is found in **Genesis 9:1-17**. Read the passage and mark the key words: **covenant**, **descendants**, and **sign**.

- What big event has just taken place? _____
- Who is initiating the covenant? God or Noah? _____

- What is the vow that God makes (verse 11)? _____
  _____

- God is making the covenant between Noah and _____
  _____

- God gives Noah a sign of the covenant. What is the sign (verse 13)?
  _____

God's Covenants: Noah

Draw a picture of the sign that God gives of His covenant to Noah:

Remember we learned that often a sign and a sacrifice accompany a covenant. We just found that God placed the rainbow in the sky as a reminder of His covenant. But was there a sacrifice?

Go to **Genesis 8:20-21**.

Was there a sacrifice? _____ What was sacrificed? _____
_____

God entered into covenant with Noah and promised that He would never again destroy the earth with a flood. And He made this covenant to Noah and to all of the generations to follow. Do you know that this includes us?! So God's covenant to Noah applies to us as well.

✢ Has God kept His promise? _____

God's Covenants: Noah

Will God continue to keep this promise? Let's look at **2 Peter 3:10**:

"But the day of the Lord will come as a thief; in which the heavens shall pass away with a great noise, and the elements shall be dissolved with fervent _____, and the earth and the works that are therein shall be _____ up."

According to God's Word, will God send another flood to destroy the earth when He returns? _____ According to this passage, how will the earth be destroyed? _____

So will God ever break His word? _____

Isn't it neat to know that God can remember His promise and He will be faithful to them?!

~ABRAHAM~

The first covenant we saw in the Bible was between God and Noah and all future generations. Let's look at the second covenant to be made.

> Read **Genesis 15** and mark key words: **Abram, God, descendants, covenant.**

Here we have God making covenant with a man named Abram (who later came to be named Abraham).

- Abram has what problem (verse 2)? _____
- God promises Abram (verse 4): _____
  _____
- How many descendants will Abram have (verse 5)? _____
  _____

God is promising to give Abram a child of his own and more descendants than he can count! Notice that God also promises Abraham a land for his descendants. In fact, in Genesis 15:18 God even gives specific directions for this land. We'll come back to this later.

Look at **verses 9-10**. What is done after God makes His promise to Abram? _____
_____
What is sacrificed? _____
_____

Do you remember that a sacrifice was the covenant-maker saying, "if I break my word, may I be destroyed as these animals were destroyed"? Let's look a little closer at this.

Verse 17   Something appears in front of Abram. What is it? _____
_____

Did you know that the image of fire often symbolizes God? Look up the following verses to get some more background on this:

Exodus 3:2-4   God speaks to Moses from what? _____

Exodus 13:22   God led the Children of Israel with what? _____
_____

Exodus 19:18   God's presence on Mt. Sinai looks like what? _____
_____

So when the smoking oven and flaming torch appeared before Abram, it was the presence of God visible to Abram as a sign of the covenant. God is literally moving through the pieces of the sacrifice, telling Abram that He is making a promise that He intends to keep!

Does God keep this covenant to Abram? Let's find out. Look up **Genesis 21:1-8**.
- How old was Abraham when his son was born? _____
- What does Abraham name his son? _____
- What was it that God had promised to Abram? _____
- So did God keep his promise to Abram? _____

~JACOB: ABRAHAM'S GRANDSON~

We saw God make a covenant with Abraham to give him a son. We saw that God literally passed through the sacrifice to show that He was initiating this promise. And we saw that God kept his promise to Abraham! But remember, God promised that Abraham would have more descendants than the stars in the sky. So this means that God's promise to Abraham would affect the generations to come. With that in mind, let's look at Abraham's grandson, Jacob.

Jacob's life was full of lots of ups and downs. He worked for years to marry the woman he loved only to be tricked into marrying her sister. He tricked his brother into giving up his inheritance, only to then have to flee from his family. But God met Jacob in a very special way and entered into covenant with him too!

> Go to Genesis 28:10-20 and mark the following key words: **Jacob, God, descendants, promise/vow.**

Verse 10   Where is Jacob? _____

Verse 12   Describe the dream that he has: _____
_____
_____

God's Covenants: Jacob

Take a minute here to draw what you imagine Jacob's dream looked like:

Verse 13-15   Fill in the words that God spoke to Jacob in his dream:

"I am the Lord, the God of _____ and the God of

_____; the _____ on which you lie, I will give it to you and to your

_____. Your _____ shall also be like the dust of the

earth, and you shall spread out to the west and to the east and to the north

and to the south; and in you and in your _____ shall all the

families of the earth be blessed."

What is God promising Jacob? _____

Do you remember what God promised to Jacob's grandfather, Abraham (Go back to **Genesis 15:17-18**)? _____

God's promise to Abraham is extending to his grandson, Jacob!

In fact as a sign of this covenant, God changes Jacob's name. Look at **Genesis 35:10** to find out what his new name is: _____

In the moment that God renames Jacob, He also reminds him of their covenant. Go to **verses 11-12** to hear God's reminder:

God also said to him, "I am God _____; Be fruitful and multiply; a _____ and a company of nations will come from you, and _____ shall come forth from you. And the _____ which I gave to _____ and _____, I will give it to you, and I will give the _____ to your _____ after you."

God calls Himself *God Almighty*. This is His name: ***El Shaddai***. It's interesting to see that Jacob's new name, Israel, contains the same Hebrew root as El Shaddai. This literally marks Jacob, and all his descendants that will follow as God's people! Is this cool or what?

God's Covenants: Jacob

So let's find out if God really does He keep his promise to Israel for descendants and a land!

Genesis 35:23-28 lists the sons of Israel. List them here:

1. _____
2. _____
3. _____
4. _____
5. _____
6. _____
7. _____
8. _____
9. _____
10. _____
11. _____
12. _____

So obviously, God continued to fulfill his promise to give Abraham descendants! But what about His promise for a land? Remember that He promised them both a large territory of land for the descendants? We'll see that happen as we continue to study.

God's Covenants: Children of Israel

CHILDREN OF ISRAEL: PEOPLE OF COVENANT

We've learned about God's covenant to Abraham and his grandson, Jacob, to give them descendants and a land. We've seen God be faithful to His promises to both of them. We also learned that Jacob's new name, Israel, is part of God's name, El Shaddai. This is going to become even more significant as we learn about Jacob's descendants.

Jacob had 12 sons who came to be called the 12 tribes of Israel. These 12 tribes became the people known as the Israelites. Read **Exodus 1:1-14** and answer the following questions:

- Jacob's sons and descendants have moved to _____
- What happens when a new king comes to power? _____
_____

As the Israelites are forced to work as Pharaoh's slaves, they cry out to God for deliverance. Read **Exodus 2:24-25** and fill in the blanks below to find out if God hears them:

"So God heard their _____; and God _____ His _____ with _____, _____, and _____. And God saw the sons of _____, and God took notice of them."

Isn't that exciting!? God remembered what He's been promising all these years and He's getting ready to move!

Read **Exodus 3:1-10** and find out who God's going to use to deliver His chosen people from their slavery in Egypt: _____

31

God's Covenants: Children of Israel

Jump over to **Exodus 6:6-8** to find out why God is going to deliver His people:

"I am the _____, and I will _____ you out from under the burdens of the Egyptians, and I will _____ you from their bondage. I will also _____ you with an outstretched arm and with great judgments. Then I will take you for My _____, and I will be your God; and you shall know that I am the Lord your God, who brought you out from under the burdens of the Egyptians. And I will bring you to the _____ which I swore to give to _____, _____, and _____ and I'll give it to you for a _____; I am the Lord."

Why does God want to deliver the people of Israel? _____
_____
Where is God planning to take them after He delivers them? _____

Is God faithful to deliver the Israelites? Read **Exodus 12:33-41** and answer the questions below:
Are the Israelites allowed to leave Egypt? _____
How long had they been in bondage? _____

The Children of Israel did not have a very easy time once they got out of Egypt. They struggled with obedience to God and delayed their entry into the Promised Land. But look at **Joshua 11:23** and you'll find that through Moses and Joshua's leadership, the Israelites do inhabit the land of Canaan that God promised to Abraham!

"Joshua took the whole land, according to all that the Lord had spoken to Moses..."

We've learned about several covenants God made in the Old Testament with certain people. Let's list them here:

	Noah	Abraham	Jacob
What was promised?			
Sign of the covenant:			
Does God fulfill His promise?			

Law: The Old Covenant

THE LAW:
GOD'S COVENANT TO HIS CHOSEN PEOPLE

Because the Israelites were God's chosen people, God entered into another covenant with them. This covenant bestowed many privileges on them but it also required some things from them. In this section, we're going to learn about this covenant, often called the **Old Covenant** or the **Covenant of the Law**. This is a very specific covenant that God entered into with the Children of Israel.

Let's review who the Children of Israel were.
- They were the descendants of whom? _____
- They had been enslaved in what country? _____
  For how long? _____
- Who was the man who God used to lead them out of slavery? _____

Do you know why God chose the Israelites to be His? Was there anything special about them? Can you think of any reason why God would choose the Israelites to be His people?
_____
_____

Law: The Old Covenant

Read **Deuteronomy 7:6-9**.

Was there anything special about the Israelites? (verse 7) _____

_____

Why did God choose them? (verse 8) _____

_____

What does God call the Israelites? (verse 6) _____

_____

Isn't that incredible? There was nothing special about the Israelites; nothing that made them deserve God's love for them. He chose to love them and take care of them!

After the Israelites left Egypt, God provided and cared for their every need. He provided water in the desert, rained down food on them every morning, healed their injuries and even kept their shoes from wearing out! Can you tell that these are God's special friends!? But it gets even better!

God, once again, enters into a covenant. This time, it is with an entire group of people.

> Read **Exodus 19:1-9** and mark the following key words:
>
> **Lord, Covenant, Nation.**

Law: The Old Covenant

✦ How much time has passed since the Children of Israel left Egypt?
_____

✦ Where are they? _____

God reminds the Israelites of what He's done for them in Egypt. In **Exodus 19:4**, it says that He "_____ them on eagle's _____" and He brought them to Himself. Keep going…. what else does God say?

Verse 5   'Now then, if you will indeed _____ My voice and keep My _____, then you shall be My own _____ among all the peoples, for all the earth is _____; and you shall be to Me a _____ of priests and a _____ nation.'

Notice that God promises 3 things if they will be obedient and keep His covenant:

   a. _____
   b. _____
   c. _____

How do the Children of Israel respond to God's call to obedience? Look in verse 8. _____
_____

God goes on to tell them that He will show them a sign of this covenant. What did this sign look like?

   Verse 18   "Mount Sinai was all in _____ because the _____ descended upon it in _____; and its _____ ascended like the smoke of a _____, and the whole mountain quaked violently.'"

So what was the sign that God gave them? _____

Law: The Old Covenant

Draw a picture here of what you imagine Mt. Sinai looked like when God's glory rested on it!

Law: The Old Covenant

We learned that there are 3 things that God will do for Israel, but what do they need to do? Look at **Exodus 20**. What does God give to Moses for the Israelites to follow? _____

The Children of Israel agreed to follow God's laws for them, but it is not long before they break their promise to obey God!

The Ten Commandments laid out specific laws that the Israelites must follow. When they broke those laws, they were required to go before the priest so that he could offer a sacrifice on their behalf. The blood of the animal that was sacrificed would wash their sins away and make them innocent. . . until they sinned again and another sacrifice would need to be made!

In **Deuteronomy 4**, Moses reminds the Israelites of the covenant. In fact, he even tells them what will happen in the future if they continue to disobey God.

Verse 26 "I call heaven and earth to witness against you today, that you shall surely _____ quickly from the _____ where you are going over the Jordan to possess it. You shall not _____ long on it, but shall be utterly _____. And the Lord will _____ you among the _____, and you shall be left few in number among the _____, where the Lord shall drive you."

So did God require obedience from the Children of Israel? _____
Will He punish them for their disobedience? _____

But look at what He will also do!

Verse 29 But from there you will _____ the Lord your _____, and you will _____ Him if you search for Him with _____ your _____ and all your _____.

Law: The Old Covenant

Verse 31 For the Lord your God is a compassionate God; He will not fail you nor destroy you nor _____ the _____ with your fathers which He swore to them.

So will God give up on His end of the covenant just because the Israelites were disobedient to their end? _____

Look at **2 Timothy 2:13**. Copy it here: _____
_____

What does this tell us about God? _____
_____

So the Children of Israel entered into a covenant with God and promised to be obedient to His laws. But they can not be obedient to God. Why not?

Look at **Romans 7:18-19**--

"For I know that nothing good dwells in me, that is, in my flesh; for the wishing is present in me; but the doing of the good is not. For the good that I wish, I do not do; but I practice the very evil that I do not wish. "

Read **Romans 3:23** and write it out below:
_____

So we can want to be obedient, we can desire to be faithful to God—but is it possible for us to do it on our own? _____

Law: The Old Covenant

Take a minute and think about <u>*your*</u> level of obedience. Are you like the Children of Israel—you want to be obedient but you have a hard time doing it? Why?

_____

_____

We need some help to be obedient, don't we? That's where a **New Covenant** comes into play! God sees that we need some help and He puts a new law into place for us.

Fasten your seatbelts and get ready to find out about the new way of life that God has made available so that we can *all* be His chosen people—not just the Israelites!

Grace: The New Covenant

THE NEW COVENANT
FOR GOD'S ADOPTED CHILDREN

Before we start looking at this New Covenant, let's review what the Old Covenant was.

- ✦ Who set up the Old Covenant? _____
- ✦ Who was the mediator of this covenant? _____
- ✦ What were the rules of this covenant? _____
  _____
- ✦ Where were the rules written? _____
- ✦ What did this covenant require? _____
- ✦ What was God's reason for choosing the Israelites? _____
  _____

So the Old Covenant required obedience and sacrifice for sins. Because the people were sinful, they could not come near to God. They had to have a priest who would make the sacrifices on their behalf. They could not approach God on their own. But God is a Covenant-making God and He's not done fulfilling His promises. Keep going to find out what God's going to do next!

As the Children of Israel continued to disobey God's commands, they were punished. Eventually the kingdom that was strong and prosperous under King David, was divided and the people became captives, or slaves, of other people. But even through this time, God did not forget His promises to His people. God spoke to His people through a prophet, Jeremiah, and made a very important new promise to them.

Grace: The New Covenant

Read **Jeremiah 31:31-33** and then fill it in below:

" 'Behold, days are coming', declares the Lord, 'when I will make a _____ _____ with the house of _____ and with the house of _____, not like the _____ which I made with their fathers in the day I took them by the hand to bring them out of the land of Egypt, My _____ which they _____, although I was a husband to them,' declares the Lord. 'But this is the _____ which I will make with the house of _____ after those days,' declares the Lord, 'I will put my _____ within them, and on their _____ I will write it; and I will be their _____, and they shall be My _____.' "

✢ What is God promising Israel? _____
✢ What will this new covenant do? _____
_____

Do you remember that when God gave Moses and the Children of Israel His law, it was written on stone tablets? But here God is promising to write the laws of His new covenant on the people's hearts!

But how will He do this? Read **Isaiah 9:6-7, Malachi 3:1** and **Luke 1:67-79**. Can you tell what is coming? Who is going to change everything? _____

Grace: The New Covenant

So we see that God is going to send Jesus to change everything and initiate a New Covenant. But why? Why did God even give the Old Law if He was going to start a new one?

Look at **Galatians 3:24-29**:

"Therefore the _____ has become our _____ to lead us to _____, that we may be justified by faith. But now that _____ has come, we are no longer under a _____."

What is a tutor? Use your dictionary to look up this word and fill in the definition here:
_____

So what was the purpose of the old law? _____
_____

Why do we need a Savior? _____

The Children of Israel were required to obey a law that they could not obey. They were not strong enough, or righteous enough all by themselves to obey God's law. They would fail any time they tried! And we do too!

So God gave us a New Law---a new covenant to take the place of the Old Covenant!

Grace: The New Covenant

God promised to send a Messiah, a Savior, to implement this New Covenant. Let's make some connections between this promise and some of the other promises that God has made.

Go back to **Genesis 35**. Remember that God had changed Jacob's name to Israel? He also promised him a land and descendants, right? Look at verse 11 again and write it here:

_____
_____
_____

What did God say would come from Jacob's family? _____
_____

So not only did God promise him descendants and a land, He promised that some of those descendants would be kings! Let's find out if that happened.

Grace: The New Covenant

Go to **Matthew 1:2-17**. We're going to use this chapter to complete the genealogy below:

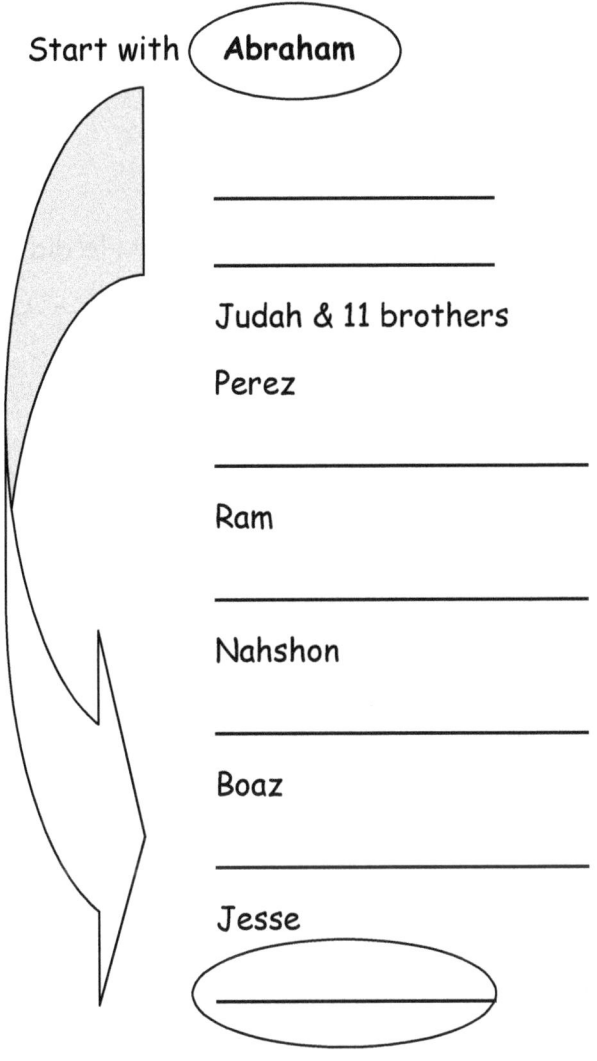

Start with **Abraham**

_____
_____
Judah & 11 brothers
Perez
_____
Ram
_____
Nahshon
_____
Boaz
_____
Jesse
_____

So who is the king that came from Abraham's family? _____

So God DID keep His promise to bring a king through Jacob's family! But guess what? It doesn't stop there! Keep going……

45

Grace: The New Covenant

Start with **David** and keep reading. Count down 28 generations.

- Who was the last King that was born into this family? _____
- So did God keep His promise to Jacob that his descendants would be kings? _____

The King of Kings came from Jacob's line!

So our God is a faithful, covenant-making and covenant-keeping God! He did not forget the promises He made hundreds of years ago to Abraham and Jacob, did He? We see that Jesus is the fulfillment of that promise!

Now let's take a closer look at what it was that Jesus came to do for us. **Matthew 1:21** tells of the angel visiting Mary to tell her about her pregnancy. Write verse 21 here: _____
_____

Now go to **Matthew 2:6** and fill in the blanks here:

"And you, _____, land of _____, are by no means least among the leaders of _____; for out of _____ shall come forth a _____, who will _____ my _____ _____."

- So what is Jesus' mission? What is His reason for coming to earth?
_____

We know that He did save His people from their sins. But how?

46

Grace: The New Covenant

Philippians 2:8 tells us that Jesus became obedient and did what? _____
_____

Fill in **Hebrews 9:28** below:

"So _____ also, having been offered _____ to bear the _____ of many, shall appear a second time for _____ without reference to sin, to those who eagerly _____ Him."

Jesus came and died for us so that we could have the gift of salvation. But what does this mean for covenant?

✢ Up until this point God's covenant has been for whom? _____

Everything we've read and learned has shown us that God made covenant with the Jews, the Children of Israel. So does that involve us? _____.

Keep reading though—God is about to do something new!

"I will call those who were not My people, My people."
~Romans 9:25

In **Luke 2:32**, Jesus is called the "light of revelation to the Gentiles", and the glory of Israel. What does this mean? What is a Gentile? _____
_____

Galatians 3:13-14: "Christ _____ us from the curse of the ____, having become a curse for us—for it is written, 'Cursed is everyone who hangs on a tree'"—in order that in _____ _____ the blessing of _____ might come to the _____ so that we might receive the _____ of the Spirit through _____."

- ✢ What are we redeemed from? _____
- ✢ According to this passage, why did Christ come? _____
_____

Read and fill in the following passages….

Romans 8:14-16:

"For all who are being led by the _____ of _____, these are _____ of God. For you have not received a spirit of slavery leading to fear again, but you have received a spirit of _____ as _____ by which we cry out, 'Abba! _____!' The Spirit Himself bears witness with our spirit that we are _____ of God."

Galatians 4:7:

"Therefore you are no longer a _____, but a _____; and if a _____, then an _____ through God."

Ephesians 1:7

"In Him we have _____ through His _____, the _____ of our trespasses, according to the riches of His grace, which He lavished upon us."

Ephesians 2:12-13

"Remember that you were at that time _____ from _____, excluded from the commonwealth of _____, and _____ to the _____ of _____ having no hope and without _____ in the world. But now in Christ Jesus you who formerly were _____ off have been brought _____ by the _____ of Christ."

So Christ's mission in coming to earth and dying for us was to create a new covenant. This new covenant would include Gentiles, people who were not included in the first covenant. That's us! Jesus came so that we could be included into His family!

Think about what you've been given by being adopted into Jesus' family. Take a minute to write a prayer of praise and thanksgiving for what He's done for you: _____

_____

_____

_____

_____

~OUR PART IN THE NEW COVENANT~

So we've seen what Jesus came to do for us in this new covenant, but what is our part in it?

Read **Hebrews 10:16-23**.

According to this passage, we were given what? _____

_____

✤ What is boldness? Use your dictionary to look it up and write the definition here:

_____

_____

_____

So because we have boldness, what should we do? _____

_____

_____

Isn't this amazing?! If we accept the work that Jesus Christ did for us and we allow Him into our heart, we will be adopted children of the Most High God. And we don't need to waver or worry about losing what we've been given. Why? Because "He who promised is faithful"! Our God can be trusted and He won't forget His promises!

Our Part in Covenant

So if you are in covenant with an Almighty God, what does this mean about your relationship with others? What does this mean about the purpose in your friendships? Look back at **Hebrews 10:24-25** and fill it in below:

"Let us consider how to stimulate _____ _____ to love and good deeds, not forsaking our own assembling together, as is the habit of some, but _____ one another and all the more, as you see the day drawing near."

✢ What is our responsibility to each other? _____
_____

Do you remember that one of the traits of covenant was that you would defend and protect not just the person you are in covenant with, but also their friends & family? So if I'm in covenant with God and you're in covenant with God, then we should encourage and defend all those who God is in covenant with!

Think about the way you handle your friendships. Now that you know that you're in covenant with God's friends, how do you treat other people? Take a minute to think about this and write down your thoughts below:

_____
_____
_____
_____

CONCLUSION

We started our study on covenant by looking at the friendship of Jonathan and David. We know that they cut covenant with each other because they loved each other and desired to put the other one ahead of themselves. Let's look at the conclusion of their story now.

Do you remember what Jonathan asked of David in **1 Samuel 20**? Go back to verses 14-15 and fill in what Jonathan wanted from David: _____
_____

Keep this in mind! We're going to jump ahead a little in the story of Jonathan & David.

David has had to flee because of Saul's violent anger towards him. He lives constantly on the run trying to stay hidden from this mad man. In the mean time, David is successful in defeating many of Israel's enemies. God gives him favor and his reputation spreads throughout Israel. This of course only does more to anger Saul.

In **1 Samuel 31**, we see that the Philistines again come to fight the Israelites and Saul leads his army into battle. Saul's army loses and rather than be captured by the enemy, Saul kills himself by falling on his own sword.

Go to **1 Samuel 31:8**. What do the Philistines find the next day?
_____

Conclusion

- Is Jonathan one of the 3 sons that they find?! Look at verse 2 to see if Jonathan had gone with his father to fight? What did you find?
  _____

- So has our heroic prince died in battle? _____

What do you think will happen when David hears the news of his friend's death? Go to **2 Samuel 1:1-15** to read about what happens.

- Who tells David that Jonathan & Saul have died? _____
- What does this man say happened? _____
- Why would this man want to take responsibility for killing Saul? _____
  _____
- What is David's response to the Amalekite? _____

Wow! David's response was not at all what the Amalekite expected! The Amalekite lied and took credit for the death of King Saul and his sons. David kills this man for taking the life of God's anointed. Despite all of the wrong Saul had done to him, David was still honorable and loyal to the covenant he was in with Jonathan.

Now look at what David has to say for Jonathan:

> "O my dear brother Jonathan, I'm crushed by your death.
> Your friendship was a miracle-wonder, love far exceeding anything
> I've known— or ever hope to know." (*The Message*)
> ~2 Samuel 1:26

Conclusion

What an emotional scene! Rather than be glad and rejoice that the man seeking to kill him is dead, David grieves the loss of his best friend and avenges the man who said he had murdered them!

So is that the end of the story? Are we going to end such a beautiful story of covenant friendship on such a sad note? No, there is still a happily-ever-after! Take a look at what David does a little later.

> Go to **2 Samuel 9** and read the entire chapter. Mark the key words: **kindness, Jonathan, Mephibosheth**

Now let's answer a few questions about what has happened in this passage:
- Who is Mephibosheth? _____
- What is wrong with him? _____
- Why does David want to see him? _____
_____

This is covenant! David is seeking out any member of Jonathan's family who he can bless.
- Look at verse 7, what is it that David is going to give to Mephibosheth? _____
_____
_____

Mephibosheth was scared of David. He expected David to kill any and all of Saul's relatives since Saul had been David's enemy. But David did not seek any revenge for the way he'd been treated by Saul, did he? In fact, he chose instead to honor his covenant with

Jonathan by blessing Jonathan's son!

Isn't this a picture of what God does for us? In the same way that Mephibosheth was crippled, we also were crippled in our sin until Jesus stepped in. And now because of what He did for us on the cross, we are allowed to come and eat at the table of the King of Kings! Isn't God awesome?

Take a minute to think about this and as you do, write a prayer of thanksgiving and worship to God for the way He has adopted you into His family and honored the covenant He made with us through Christ.

_____

_____

_____

_____

_____

_____

Conclusion

Wow! You've learned a lot about covenant, haven't you? As we close our study, write down your thoughts to the following questions.

✟ What is something that you learned that you never knew before? _____
_____
_____
_____
_____

✟ How has covenant changed your relationship with God? _____
_____
_____
_____
_____

✟ How has covenant changed your relationships with others? _____
_____
_____
_____
_____

Lightning Source UK Ltd.
Milton Keynes UK
UKHW030224081222
413505UK00001B/12